THE AFRICAN LION

BY LISA OWINGS

BELLWETHER MEDIA · MINNEAPOLIS, MN

Jump into the cockpit and take flight with Pilot Books. Your journey will take you on high-energy adventures as you learn about all that is wild, weird, fascinating, and fun!

This edition first published in 2012 by Bellwether Media, Inc.

No part of this publication may be reproduced in whole or in part without written permission of the publisher. For information regarding permission, write to Bellwether Media, Inc., Attention: Permissions Department, 5357 Penn Avenue South, Minneapolis, MN 55419.

Library of Congress Cataloging-in-Publication Data

Owings, Lisa.
The African lion / by Lisa Owings.
    p. cm. – (Pilot books. Nature's deadliest)
Includes bibliographical references and index.
Summary: "Fascinating images accompany information about the African lion. The combination of high-interest subject matter and narrative text is intended for students in grades 3 through 7"–Provided by publisher.
ISBN 978-1-60014-740-1 (hardcover : alk. paper)
1. Lion–Juvenile literature. I. Title.
QL737.C23O95 2012
599.757–dc23   2011029432

Printed in the United States of America, North Mankato, MN.

010112   1204

CONTENTS

The Rufiji Man-Eater

Thirteen-year-old Amir Legaza ate dinner with his mother outside their hut in southern Tanzania. After the meal, Amir went to bed while his mother finished the daily chores. When Amir woke up the next morning, his mother was gone. He frantically searched for her, following a trail of bright fabric scraps through the bush. The scraps were pieces of his mother's dress. And they were soaked in blood.

Amir's heart raced. He hoped to find his mother in time to save her. But he was too late. Amir's mother had been eaten by a ferocious African lion. She was the lion's first taste of human flesh.

It wasn't long before Fatuma Magaila met a fate similar to Amir's. She witnessed the same lion violently **maul** her husband to death. Soon after the attack, Fatuma visited her parents. She talked with them late into the night, unaware that the Rufiji man-eater was waiting outside.

Once Fatuma and her parents were asleep, the lion climbed the wall of the hut and sprang through the grass roof. Fatuma watched in horror as the same lion that had killed her husband attacked her mother. Her father tried to fight it off, but he was no match for the 400-pound (180-kilogram) beast. The lion killed Fatuma's father and dragged her mother out of the hut. Fatuma survived by staying quiet and still.

The Man-Eaters of Tsavo

Two lions in the Tsavo region of Kenya were famous for man-eating. These lions killed and devoured at least 35 railroad workers in 1898. Today, you can see these lions' bodies on display at the Field Museum in Chicago, Illinois.

The Rufiji man-eater continued to hunt farmers along the Rufiji River. Many farmers abandoned their homes and crops to escape the lion. They crossed to the other side of the river where they thought they would be safe. But the lion followed them. It was still hungry for human flesh. By the time hunters finally killed the lion, it was thought to have eaten about 50 people.

The Rufiji man-eater was a young male lion. He was large and strong but had a painful broken tooth. Some experts believe this may have caused him to seek easy prey. Humans were easier to kill and softer to eat than zebras or gazelles. Others believe the lion learned to hunt humans from other man-eaters.

All-They-Can-Eat

African lions can eat up to 75 pounds (34 kilograms) of meat at one time. Then they can go for a week without food

An Expert Killer

Lions have roamed the earth for more than two million years. The African lion has **evolved** into one of the deadliest animals in the world. It is the second-largest feline after the tiger. Male lions can weigh more than 500 pounds (227 kilograms). Their size and strength allow them to kill large prey such as buffalo, elephants, and hippopotamuses.

Lionesses are lighter, faster, and more **agile** than males. They run in short bursts and can reach speeds over 40 miles (64 kilometers) per hour. They are quick enough to catch zebras and gazelles.

Africa

N
W · E
S

African lion territory = ☐

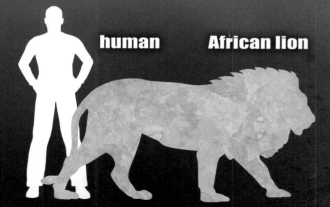

human　　**African lion**

The African Lion's Hunting Tools
- **Excellent vision, especially at night**
- **Strong sense of smell**
- **Sharp sense of hearing**
- **Padded paws for silent walking**
- **Tan coat to blend in with surroundings**
- **Curved teeth and claws for seizing prey**

African lions live in groups called **prides**. Living in groups makes it easier for lions to defend their territory, reproduce, and hunt successfully. Lions are **carnivores**. The lionesses in a pride do almost all of the hunting. When hunting as a group, two or three lionesses wait near a herd of prey. Others surround the herd and chase the animals toward the waiting lionesses.

When the prey comes close, the lionesses attack. They leap onto the back or neck of their victim. Their sharp teeth and claws sink into the animal's flesh. They **suffocate** it by crushing its **windpipe** or clamping its **muzzle** in their jaws. Then the lionesses feast. They rip out and eat the internal organs first. They eat as much of the kill as they can before the male lions come to claim their share.

Male lions sometimes help the lionesses hunt large prey. However, their main job is to **defend** the pride's territory. Lions often rule the pride as a **coalition** of two or three. The coalition fights other **males** that try to take over the pride. The fight for the pride is fierce and can turn deadly.

When a new coalition of lions takes over a pride, they try to kill all the young cubs in the pride. They do not want to help raise and protect other lions' cubs. Many cubs are killed this way. Lionesses can defend their cubs only if they outnumber the lions. All prides will eventually be taken over by younger, stronger males.

Mane Reasons

A lion's mane has many functions. It makes the lion look bigger, and it helps protect his face and neck during a fight. Scientists believe the mane also attracts females. In fact, research shows that lionesses prefer dark manes.

African Lion Attacks

Most African lions have learned to stay away from humans. However, if a lion feels threatened, it will attack. Lions usually attack a person's head or neck. A large lion can fit an entire human head in its powerful jaws.

Some lions hunt humans for food. Lions usually do not eat humans unless they cannot eat or catch their usual prey. Injured or sick lions may find humans easier to catch than other prey. Children, elderly people, and sick or disabled people are the most likely victims. Attacks on humans also increase during the rainy season. Flooding often forces lions to seek higher ground away from their regular food source. Most frighteningly, man-eating lions often teach their cubs and even other lions to hunt humans. This can cause generations of fatal attacks.

Open Wide

A lion can open its jaws up to 1 foot (30 centimeters) wide. Its longest teeth can grow up to 3 inches (7.6 centimeters) long.

People who live near lions can prevent attacks by understanding lion behavior. Lions rarely attack people in groups. This means people should not travel alone, especially at night. People must be careful if they are traveling with pets or young children. They could be viewed as prey.

Villagers need to pay close attention to reports of what lions in the area are doing. They should take care to avoid **dens**, mating lions, and lionesses with cubs. Tourists on **safaris** should stay with a guide and never get out of their vehicle.

If you think a lion will attack, maintain eye contact and back away slowly. Do not run. If you do, the lion will consider you prey. Stand up tall and make a lot of noise to try and scare the lion away. Toss any food you have to the lion. If it starts to charge, protect your face and neck. Stand your ground. If you appear strong, the lion may leave you alone.

African lions are in danger of becoming **extinct**. Lions once stalked the plains of North America, Africa, Asia, and Europe. Today, lions live mainly in Africa's nature preserves and national parks. African lions face a variety of threats. Farmers kill lions to protect their livestock, and hunters kill lions for sport.

Lions have been one of the most feared and admired animals since ancient times. Today, they draw tourists from around the world to the savannahs of Africa. Many people are working to save these deadly predators. They believe violent attacks can be prevented so the king of the jungle can continue its mighty reign.

Attack Facts

- Between 1932 and 1947, lions killed 1,500 people in the Njombe district of Tanzania.

- Between 1990 and 2005, more than 560 people were killed and more than 300 injured by lion attacks in Tanzania.

- In eastern Africa, lions kill more than 120 people each year.

21

Glossary

agile—able to move the body quickly and with ease

carnivores—animals that eat meat

coalition—a small group that rules; a few lions form a coalition to rule over a pride; members of a coalition are equal in rank.

dens—sheltered places where lionesses give birth to their young

evolved—changed and developed slowly over time

extinct—no longer living as a species

maul—to injure with deep wounds

muzzle—the nose and mouth of an animal

prides—groups of lions, lionesses, and cubs; most prides have about 15 members.

safaris—trips to see or hunt wildlife in their natural habitats

suffocate—to prevent an animal from breathing

windpipe—the tube through which some animals breathe; the windpipe runs from the throat to the lungs.

At the Library

Bourke, Anthony, and John Rendall. *Christian the Lion*. New York, N.Y.: Henry Holt and Co., 2009.

Hapka, Catherine. *African Cats: A Lion's Pride*. New York, N.Y.: Disney Editions, 2011.

Joubert, Beverly, and Dereck Joubert. *Face to Face with Lions*. Washington, D.C.: National Geographic, 2008.

On the Web

Learning more about African lions is as easy as 1, 2, 3.

1. Go to www.factsurfer.com.

2. Enter "African lions" into the search box.

3. Click the "Surf" button and you will see a list of related Web sites.

With factsurfer.com, finding more information is just a click away.

The images in this book are reproduced through the courtesy of: Gracie Eppard, front cover, p. 17; Eric Gevaert, pp. 4-5; Ron Kimball / KimballStock, p. 7; Eric Isselée, pp. 8-9; Martin Harvey / Photolibrary, p. 11; Mitsuaki Iwago / Minden Pictures, pp. 12-13; Ken & Michelle Dyball / Masterfile, pp. 14-15; Fabian von Poser / Photolibrary, p. 18; Mogens Trolle, p. 19; Klein-Hubert / KimballStock, pp. 20-21.